JASON ROBERTS

The TimeLordz Movement

First edition

ISBN: 979-8-218-12389-5

This book was professionally typeset on Reedsy.
Find out more at reedsy.com

Contents

Preface

The TimeLordz Movement is a hope. It's a way for an average person to tip the scales in humanity's favor for more equality and a more technologically advanced civilization in the near future. To explain the TimeLordz Movement simply, "A person provides food, shelter, water, and electricity to a gifted and fierce individual, thereby allowing this recruit to spend all of their time on doing something beneficial for humanity."

I have been studying and analyzing the world for the past twenty five years. I am a man in his early forties who has seen and experienced many things. I have spent a lot of time trying to find answers on how society operates, how and why everything is set up the way it is. The TimeLordz Movement is the product of my life, experience and twenty five years of in depth analysis and research. I put all the pieces of the puzzle together and then came up with a solution to all of our problems and shortcomings. Time. In this book I will go over all of my insights on our time restraints and give many solutions. By the end of the book you will have a better understanding of many things in modern society. This is important for understanding the core fundamentals of being a TimeLord. You will soon see things more clearly and see that all we need is more Time to improve the world. The strength is inside humanity, we just have to free up and give some gifted people more free time.I will carve the first trail and illuminate the path towards being a Timelord. I hope some of you decide to walk with me.

1

Time

The single most important and precious thing in our short lives is time. Without time we can't do anything. With infinite time, there are infinite possibilities and outcomes. Time is so ingrained into our current society and day to day lives, yet many fail to see the grand implications of time. "He who controls time and can give it freely to others can truly change the future of humanity"

In every human life,there are many things that each individual must do to survive. Each of these tasks requires time and life to accomplish. I call these survival tasks gates. Gate 1 = Food Gate 2 = Shelter Gate 3 = water Gate 4 = energy/electricity. If a person can open all these gates for someone else, than that individual will have all of his time available for more important or specialized tasks. I think inventors and innovators are a good path to go down, but there are many possibilities.

Opening these survival gates are not an easy thing to do for yourself and others, but it is very possible if you understand all the things that are holding us back and how we are suppressed by current society operations. You will all soon be rising out of those restraints and helping to slingshot us into a better, more enjoyable, and more technologically evolved society. I will go into each control system in greater detail in future chapters.

To sum it up, all we have to do is share the basic necessities of survival with a gifted individual. This person won't have to work a normal job, giving them 5 to 7 days a week to pursue and work on their passion instead of just 1 or 2 days to do it like the rest of the working class. Such a simple time sharing done in places all over the globe would lead to a better world in less than a generation. Become a Timelord. Share some time. Give some time. Change the world.

Have you ever looked at the way the average person lives their life on a day to day basis? Have you ever looked at how many things in modern society and civilization are being done and how they operate? and function? Have you wondered why human civilization as a whole hasn't slingshotted into the future, highly technologically advanced and evolved yet? I know many of us have. We all think to ourselves, "why are we doing things this way? Why do we live like this? Surely there is a better way to speed up,evolve, and make more harmonious the human species on this planet?" We are making great improvements in many things, but at the same time, I feel our growth is stunted and meager compared to what we could have been so far. If you don't agree with my last statement, think about these statistics. According to the US Census Bureau, in 2010 there were 190 million people in the us that were of the working age group of 18–64 years old. Every year, on average, the us patent and trademark office awards around 500,000 patents for and invention. This means that only .25% of americans get a patent each year. Thats one quarter of a percent! The math tells us that there is a major problem somewhere. In fact there are many small problems and all of these problems compounded together create one giant .25% invention rate problem.

In this book I will bring to light all of the hindrances, the things that are holding us back, and all of the things that are stunting our growth. I will also give legitimate,and "everyday average person" solutions to get past all of these hindrances. We are not hopeless, helpless or powerless as individuals and definitely not as a whole. Far from it. I will light the path so we can walk down it together,easily and with understanding.

2

Get Off the Survival Time Roller Coaster

Having to spend time working for our survival needs is the biggest time thief that most of us experience. Most of us have to fight this battle during our entire adult lives. We must spend our time working or making money to pay for food,shelter,water, and electricity. Even if a person is lucky enough to purchase a home, or land, or can purchase renewable energy devices, have a garden, have livestock and animals, or have a well, all these things still require time and maintenance. Life feeds on life. Its an inescapable truth of the civilized human world and also in nature since the beginning of life itself. The circle of life continues and everything comes at a price. There is a way to get off the "survival time roller coaster", but it requires one or several people sharing their time,life, or resources with you. Otherwise your stuck on that ride. Here comes the game changer. What is most important and possibly future changing for humanity, is that the people we get off the survival time roller coaster must be highly motivated,gifted,capable,and possess what I call heart fire.(an intense burning desire that is unquenchable until their passion or mission becomes a reality) These are the type of people that have the highest probability to succeed. Our sacrifices of sharing our time,money,life,and hard earned resources will not go wasted if we become TimeLordz for these types of people. However, if we choose our candidates poorly, it would just be wasted time for all.

I personally think that inventors and innovators have the greatest potential with minimum investment vs reward. I believe this because it only takes one invention to change the world. That is just the direction that I lean towards though. Each Timelord will choose their own type of people to free up from the workforce. I know the TimeLordz Movement will be successful eventually because the true power for world change lies in the power of human passion, creativity, and imagination. All we have to do is help some talented and gifted people out with some free time.

3

Obstacles in Land Ownership

Land ownership. Part of the american dream. A person in the process of owning land instead of paying a "rent to use fee" indefinitely. Home ownership or land ownership can do great things for us. We can have plenty of rooms to share space and time with family, friends, or timelord recruits. We can use land to subdivide into many plots so we can have a mini trailer park for timelord recruits, or have gardens, livestock, energy production, timber, and firewood, the list goes on. A person being able to own his or her own property can allow them to help so many other people if they go about it the right way and also share their blessings. Its a critical step to becoming a strong TimeLord. We need to be careful with how land ownership currently works though. It can be a major time thief to the have nots and for the commercial zoned places for small businesses. If a person always has to give their portion of their paycheck to a land owner every month, then in reality, this renter is giving someone else their time spent earning the money. Monopolized commercial land works the same way. Not only does it rob the small business owner of their time, profits,and hard work, but it also holds down and stunts small business growth. These huge companies that have monopolies on major areas of commercial land are ruining small businesses, employment, and the economy. If the entrepreneur could own their own land and building, they would have more profits for expansion, more products, and be able to hire more employees and pay better wages.

Land ownership does have other less known hindrances. Don't get me wrong, Land ownership is vital and critical for a free and better equality of life for all people scenario. There are a few key things I'd like to point out so that a new, unsuspecting person doesn't get used, lied to, or put into perpetual debt slavery to a bank or mortgage lender. There are plenty of books, websites, and videos out there to help a person build credit, and to learn to understand home loans, home loan types, and amortization schedules. I recommend doing a little research, but I'll outline the darker side so that you can plan for it, and position yourself and the banks relationship to be more like a mutual usery than debt slavery.

Number one most important thing to be aware of is that all home loans and mortgages are front end loaded with interest. All of them. This means that for the first five to ten years of your mortgage payments mostly go to pay interest on the loan, home insurance, and property taxes.(depending if its a 15yr or 30yr mortgage) Only a very small amount goes toward the principle balance owed on the house. There is a way to move forward faster on your amortization calendar to pay off the house much faster and with less interest paid. You have to make principle only payments along with your normal mortgage payments. The more you can pay on the principle each month, the faster you can own your home for less cost to you.

Number two most important thing is that it is in the banks best interest and more profitable if they can keep you from getting into the halfway mark on your amortization calendar or thereby making most of your hard earned money only go toward interest to the bank. Do not, I repeat, Do not refinance. This is the "Banksters Hustle" to reset your mortgage back to its starting point, thereby causing you to have to start all over on the interest payments before you actually start paying on your house. Please do not be hustled into perpetual debt slavery. If this happens, it will just be a homeowner *scharade*, *when in fact you are just renting a home from a bank for 30 to 40 years. Please don't refinance.*

Don't let this scare you or make you think banks or mortgage lenders are bad. They are in the business of making money. Just precede with caution and do research first. Also don't let it give all refinances a bad name. There are three scenarios where a refinance could be beneficial. One is that you have a very fresh new loan and can get the interest dropped several percent. Another would be a newer 30 year loan and you change to a 15 year and get a lower interest rate. With both of these scenarios, you would end up paying less for your home or land in the long run. The third refinance scenario I like is called a "Cash Out Refinance". This would allow you to tap into the equity of your home, and get a new bigger loan that you could use for leverage, like buy some rentals, or a piece of land, or a fixer upper to flip, or make a business investment. That's all I'm going to go into in this book on loans. Be very careful and use the "mutual useries" to your advantage, and trust no one.

Buy some land or a home,apartment building,campground,rv park,or trailer park, and share some of it with people. Becoming a Timelord is easier than you think.

4

Zoning Issues

Every decent size town has a zoning and planning group. The main function of zoning is for city planning. Designating certain areas for residential, commercial, industrial, and recreation. They also help with public safety, health, pollution, property values, and fire safety. These are all important for a growing city, but we have to be careful of a few of its shortcomings. Including multi family and mobile home restrictions, favoritism, and even manipulation for personal financial gain. Zoning can be an obstacle in your path to becoming a TimeLord. We will have to work around these flaws until we can get some people trying to get things modified, improved, and updated to the modern world.

Most residential zones are only for single family dwellings. If your lucky, some areas allow for an Accessory Dwelling Unit (ADU). Also known as a mother-in-law suite,coach house, and accessory apartment. If you have a home with a big enough yard, this might be your best option for a TimeLords building. Be careful of land size requirements, easements, home size requirements, building inspectors,and permits. It could get expensive if you don't do most of the work yourself. I wish more places allowed mobile homes(trailers) and rv's. This would be the cheapest route, but... the zoning and permitting department can also be a control arm of some that don't like positive change,progress, and land sharing. Don't let this discourage you. Look for ways to get what you need in your area while still being legal and up to code. There are workarounds. You could even have several roommates, and turn the living room of your home into an office full of cubicles for recruits work space. Be creative.

While on the topic of zoning, I have to bring up a serious flaw in commercial zoning that is really stunting small business growth and creating huge corporate monopolies. Towns and cities need to start leaving a lot of the commercially zoned land only for small business entrepreneurs. We can't allow big commercial real estate companies to buy up all the land and "strip mall" it all. They will charge rent, thereby putting small businesses into a perpetual debt slavery. I'm making people aware of this so that we can create positive change and improvements in this sector one day in the future.

Industrial zoning needs some help and improvements as well. We need more grassroots type small town factories. So we are gonna have to get industrial zoning loosened up too. We need local municipalities to open some "light industrial zones" set aside for only small factory start ups and local entrepreneurs. We can't allow the industrial zones to come up for sale and be bought by rich real estate investors who are just in it to make land rent money. We need it in the hands of people that care more about other things besides money and profits. Doing this would boost all economies at the local level and also strengthen our nation as a whole. We would become more self reliant and self sufficient. A town and country that can create and produce most of the things it needs, is a fierce and strong town and country.

5

Distractions and Society Dysfunctions

In this section I want to show some areas with plenty of room for improvement and evolvement. There are many things that people like to do with their spare time to unwind and relax. I'm just gonna go into two major sectors that need some further analysis and scrutiny.

Movies and tv shows. We have come a long way in regards to cinema, tv shows and programs. There is great variety and artistic freedom. I do however want to go into how show ratings, tv station profits, and box office movie and video sales play a huge roll in the big scheme of things. TV networks and movie production companies watch the trends and watch what's most popular to their viewing audience to better choose the stuff that satisfies people and makes the most profits. This is all an integral part of entertainment and business. I bring this up because we can use this system to our advantage from a TimeLord perspective to get more movies, shows, game shows, and series more invention, innovation, and technologically advanced oriented. If we mostly watch shows about science, invention, society improvements, human culture evolving, human equality, human freedoms, etc, they would get higher ratings, thereby making these things more profitable for the companies to show. We can also make all kinds of suggestions and requests to these companies. For example, movies about good Utopias on earth, game shows and contest shows with inventing and innovating.(sort of like how we have cooking shows now) Maybe a reality show about a TimeLord that has a home with several scientists all working on inventions. These types of changes would bring a better view of the future in regards to humans moving up in the technological age.

The other topic I want to discuss is sports. Again, ratings, advertising, and profits all play a huge roll in these. I enjoy sports as entertainment also, but should we be paying athletes millions of dollars to "bounce a rubber ball on a wooden floor", "run on grass carrying a piece of leather", or "hit a ball with a stick and run around in the dirt?" When broken down into these simplified definitions, maybe people will see their importance, significance, and what they bring for humanity. These games haven't changed much since their invention. We had the Coliseum even back in Roman era. Yes they bring us entertainment,and being able to follow and cheer for certain teams. We can play a sport we enjoy. They brought us better energy drinks, work out supplements, better training methods, more athleticism, and health and nutrition education. I'm just saying that sports have reached their peak on the human evolutionary path, and it is now time to hold more important things in the spotlight. Shouldn't we be paying scientists, inventors, and innovators more money? Shouldn't they be taken care of and held in higher regard? Shouldn't they be the ones getting sponsorship and advertising deals? Shouldn't they be idolized for what they do for humanity, human evolution, and planet earth? They should be getting free housing, government and community aid, scholarships, research and development funding, and our help. It's time to transition more toward a scientific, technologically advanced, and better world for all. We can do it.

It would also be wise for some up and coming entrepreneurs to have a scientist wearing or using their invention, gear, or clothing line. We can sponsor scientists that way, and get them more intertwined with advertising and company profits. This will also get the ball rolling on "science sells". It will take some time, but things can change for the better eventually.

6

Corporate and Inventor Greed

Have you ever wondered why we are still using old methods to power a lot of our power plants? You know we have been driving internal combustion engine vehicles since the late 1800's ? You know the electric car was invented in the late 1800's also? You ever wonder why we don't have natural cures to illnesses or more cures for diseases? You ever wonder why we don't have star trek and star wars type technology currently in use? Progress in all of these things have been stunted and held back due to two reasons. One reason is no time for research and development, and number two reason is corporate and inventor greed.

I have given many solutions for our time problem. TimeLords and the sharing of time can fix all problems in society. We give people that are passionate about certain things free time, and they use that time to fight for us. Pretty simple fix.

The solution and fix to corporate greed is quite a bit more complex and harder to deal with. It can be fixed and progressed to a better way of things, but will require some effort. It will require more teamwork, selflessness, and some people giving inventions to public domain. I will first illuminate those in the dark of how the real corporate world can be. For starters, we live in a society that mostly revolves around money and finance. Keep that in mind. Many of us don't like it, but it's a reality. There are some corporations out there that perform corporate espionage and sabotage. Some buy up patents and inventions if it poses a threat to their product or would make their company uncompetitive or obsolete. Some may even commit darker deeds to keep their company profits and stock shares up and rising. It's sad but true. Such bad morals and ethics are hard to beat when a company or industry has billions of dollars. There is a few ways that a TimeLord can counteract, or circumvent such behavior. One way is trying to do more small business and grassroots shopping when possible. Another way is getting new inventions put into the free domain for public use. Getting a patent is hard and might require a lawyer, but before and during the process, an inventor and innovator can use what is called an "Affidavit" to claim property, intellectual property rights, design, date of notary,and rights for future use. Do some research on notarized legal documents. It is a lot easier than you think to create a legal binding document that could hold up in court. Of course it would be nice if we could use TimeLords time share method to free up some bright minds that would love to go to law school and fight for human equality and evolution. But until we can get a bunch of human rights lawyers, we will have to use our own paperwork, or hire a lawyer, and use the patent office. Once the intellectual property rights have been claimed, and design rights, assuming it doesn't already exist somewhere else, the person can upload all information onto the internet for shared free public use for everyone in the world. This method will get some new inventions and technology out that can't be suppressed by corporate greed.

Another way to counteract the greed problem is by starting TimeLords time shares all over the place. Eventually some inventors that are pure of heart and willing to share freely with the world will create some amazing stuff. This is a serious probability. The right people simply just need some more free time and they will invent a better world for us.

I also want to go into the healthcare and pharmaceutical industries. Perhaps the reason we don't have as many natural cures for things is because it isn't profitable if a pharmaceutical company can't patent it and corner the rights and profits of it. The same would go for disease cures and the medical profession. If we were an illness and disease free world, healthcare and pharmaceutical companies would become a lot less profitable and powerful. Think about that. Be careful of greed everywhere. I do have a solution though.

Timelords. We give some people with knowledge of medicine and the passion to help people some free time. They will come up with something eventually. They would need a license to practice medicine, but there are other options and workarounds if it has to do with religion or spiritualism, or in a private membership association. But just freeing up some activists to give them time to inform the public of bad behavior, or get petitions going for change, or talking to representatives in politics. If we free up the right kind of passionate people, they will fight for us and we can have a healthier, more evolved world one day. It just takes time.

7

Energy Creation, Affordability, and Monopolies

The main tasks to become a Timelord for others is to provide food,shelter,water,and electricity to others so they have free time. This section will be about energy and electricity. Depending on the route you choose and what situation your in, you might get your electricity from a power company, or off grid self creation. I think having both in one setup is optimal, but do what suits your needs.

I'm gonna go into Energy companies and monopolies a little bit because there are some things to be aware of. The power companies are there to make a profit. They are also there as an important part of our infrastructure, survival, and luxurious lifestyle. They keep and maintain the power stations, wires, and electric meters, so we have to "pay to play". We are lucky to have all of this, but there are a couple things to be aware of. Number one is that they determine the price per kilowatt hour. They can raise it as energy costs and operating costs rise. Number two is smart meters. There is a lot of literature, and websites to inform and educate us on the pros and cons of these "controversial" smart meters. I suggest you do some studying. To give you an important fact in regards to timelords, and keeping the lights on in your buildings, smart meters can be monitored and shut off remotely by the power company. I have heard of recent shutoffs because of high strains on the grid, not enough power, etc.

Although these instances have been rare, they are possible in the future. This is why I recommend a secondary private power station and control box from your self generated power.

I will explain several methods to have alternative self power in the event of an emergency. One way to do this, is to have an electrician install a separate breaker box in your home and run more outlets to several parts of your home, so that you have a secondary wiring and socket system. You will have to make sure you label them and color them different. You will also need a power controller, battery charger, and batteries. With this setup, you would even be in specifications with electrical building code and it wouldn't negate your home owner insurance in the event of a fire. Just make sure you use a licensed electrician and get a permit and building inspector. With this setup, you could use a gas powered generator to power your home temporarily, or even better you can have solar panels charging up your batteries. Id also incorporate some wind turbines for when the sun isn't shining. Another method is possibly a hydroelectric turbine if your lucky enough to have a creek or river. Lastly I'm going to suggest another method not as common but would be very effective. Now I have to say that you really need to do a lot of studying and research for this method, so be very careful. You can modify any internal combustion engine that doesn't have a computer to run on a "HHO" hydrogen on demand gas.(You could use an engine with a computer but you would have to reprogram the gas to air ratio controller to run it correctly). Essentially you run the engine on something very cheap. Baking soda, water, and a little electrical current running through it creating hydrogen gas. This engine can have a pulley hooked up to it, which is hooked up to a big fly wheel, which is hooked up to several alternators. Hook these alternators up to a charging controller which charges many batteries. You will have your own power station and can scale it up to suit your needs. Please be very careful and have your engine outdoors, well exhausted, and with many safety features. Hydrogen gas is explosive, and electrical shock can kill you. Proceed with extreme caution if you try this method. Very cheap fuel cost though.

If your timelords home is rural and off grid, you will be able to do all the things I previously mentioned. Use solar,wind, generator, or alternatives to charge batteries for energy storage. You will still need an electrical breaker box, wiring, charge controller, and batteries. Have the breaker box and stuff installed by a licensed electrician so you are safe from fires and losing life or home. Electricity is very dangerous. You can do some things yourself but the big stuff, go with the professional. While on the topic of "off grid" I would like to recommend ways to heat. Do lots of research, but you will find propane, kerosene, and wood burning stoves most popular. There are even some nice diesel heaters that can run on recycled cooking oil now, or even modified to run on a gas vapor of your choice. I personally have a secondary backup heat source in case one type fails. I recommend the same and stay safe and fire free. Keep electrical fire and several other types of fire extinguishers at the ready.

I'm excited to think that one day TimeLords will bring us many inventions in the energy creation sector. We just have to give some brilliant people more free time to work on stuff. They will win for us.

8

The Economic Machine

The economic machine is a critical part of life for every country in the world and the global economy as a whole. Without a proper functioning economic machine, peoples way of life and lifestyle start to degrade, less things they want are available for purchase, they can't earn a good living, and crime rates rise. I am pointing this out because as a prospective Timelord, you need to know and understand it. Not everyone can have a lot of free time. At least not until we make huge technological advances in many fields and transition into a much different way of life. So don't get the wrong idea and think that The TimeLordz Movement is about making us free as a whole. It would be catastrophic and devastating for millions of lives if the economic machines worldwide went down. The machine has to run or things aren't produced, stores aren't open,we won't have food,clothes, or entertainment, etc. This would actually backpedal our progress,technology, and evolution. We would all have to be hunters,gatherers, and farmers again. Life would suck. Think of being a Timelord more like a talent selector. You can pull several highly gifted and passionate people out of the workforce. By doing this, you give special people the time and opportunity to work on things that will benefit their country and humanity. Instead of working a forty plus hour work week job the average person could do, they can spend forty to sixty hours a week on their passion or gifts. I say this because a person doing something they love isn't really working, they are enjoying themselves. This timelording can be done to help any kind of topic,subject, or genre. Just find gifted, passionate people and they will get it done. So don't worry about "freeing humanity". We are not ready for that yet.

Not having a strong economic machine to share with the rest of the world is also counter productive. We can be strong,self sufficient, and more self reliant though. Our country, and all other countries should be striving for self reliance and fierceness. If we can produce everything that we need as a country, we become strong and able to help others if we choose. There shouldn't be supply chain issues or shortages of any kind. We also need to make sure all infrastructure type businesses and assets, including farmland and factories are owned by american citizens and loyalists. This is also why I recommended earlier in my zoning section that we need to loosen up on commercial and industrial zones in respect to grass roots businesses and factories being able to sling shot us into self sufficiency as a nation.

I would also like to make a suggestion on a solution I have from the lowering of the workforce and GDP slightly when The Timelordz Movement takes off and is in full swing in towns all across the globe. No need to fear about weakening the economic machine. There are hundreds of thousands of people from other countries that would love to come to USA and live the "American Dream". All we have to do is allow more work visas and citizenship. They can be given an ID, fingerprinted,and given a worker ID number, and they must start paying taxes as soon as they are employed. This will fill the gap of workers that Timelords has pulled out of the workforce. Not only that, it will instantly be generating tax money for public things like roads, police, medicare, food aid, social security, and paying down the national debt. It would also raise the country's GDP significantly, not to mention all the new businesses and factories opening up could use reasonably priced laborers and employees. It would also increase the housing and rental market due to higher demand. Do the math and you will see that one million extra workers paying the average 20% payroll tax would bring our nation 80 to 150 million dollars a week for taxes and public programs.(That is done on the hourly rate of $7hr up to $20hr). This makes us 4 to 8 billion tax dollars a year. So don't worry about the people that Timelords can pull out of the workforce to work on a better life for all of humanity. The gap is easily filled.

The economic machine is also a major part of the M.I.C. The military industrial complex. I will explain the M.I.C. in great detail in the next chapter, but needless to say, the economic machine and the M.I.C. are heavily intertwined and dependent upon each other. We have to be strong economically to have what we need to defend ourselves and our country politically and militarily. All the more reason to get grassroots companies and factories going up here, and getting our factories back. We also need to be doing more mining and agriculture, and research and development for better inventions for an easier and higher quality of life.

9

M.I.C.

The Military Industrial Complex. This is all of the military's factories and economy, combined with all the industry for the things civilians and military personnel need. This also includes all of the 3 letter agencies, department of defense and the pentagon. It also includes all the contractors, sub contractors, umbrella corporations, and even private businesses making products for all of these groups. Like I said earlier, the M.I.C. is heavily intertwined with the economy, and it is very important for all life in our country. Each country has their own M.I.C. Also, don't think its just an american thing. The bigger the country and the stronger its military is, the bigger their Military Industrial Complex is.

Needless to say, in a world like ours, with disputes, fighting over borders, resources, economic dominance, military dominance, invention and innovation dominance, criminal enterprise, drug and weapons trade, tyrants, and weapons of mass destruction, It is important to be a major military power. Please keep all of these things in mind when you decide to become a Timelord. The Timelordz Movement is about creating positive changes and evolving society and quality of life without creating chaos or disorder. It's about freeing brilliant people to use their gifts and free time to do good things for us and the people of the world. I have to strongly recommend extreme caution if you decide to sponsor inventors though. Some things are better left to trained professionals. However, don't let that advice discourage you. One invention can change the world. That is what The TimeLordz Movement is all about. Progressive improvement and raising our quality of life.

I do want to go into one more thing about the M.I.C. Inventions that are considered, "a threat to national security". The department of defense and the department of homeland security have an important job to do. Keep us all alive and safe as a nation. We are lucky to have them fighting for us and keeping an eye on things. There has been thousands of inventions and patents seized by these agencies for reasons of "a threat to national security". Lets be honest. We have to stay a military super power or we could lose to strong tyrants. Also there are a lot of technologies and inventions that don't need to be in the hands of the masses due to ignorance, stupidity, and uncontrolled human emotion. However, I'm willing to bet that some of these suppressed and seized inventions aren't dangerous anymore. They were probably only dangerous to a big corporation's wallet and profits. Just keep all of this in mind when someone discovers or invents something amazing. If you don't think it could harm the masses somehow, or hurt us as far as military technology competitiveness, then the best route is probably releasing it into the public domain for free use and production for all the world. Otherwise a "snake in the grass" infiltrator in one of the M.I.C. agencies might just make it disappear. I think there are some groups trying to get some of these older inventions out and released, but for now and the future, just give the invention to the world publicly for free use. It's time for a better world now. Greed will only hold us back.

10

Don't Drop Out

In the course of my life travels I have met many people that just decided to drop out of society. I too tried to drop out a few times. Most people wanna drop out because this current world and the way it operates almost seems backwards or not quite right. It's hard for them to fake it or play along. Sometimes some people stop striving for change because it seems hopeless. Some refuse to live by unjust and unrighteous rules. Some don't want money as their god. Some get sick of the day to day grind and lose hope for humanity and the future. Others become selfish and decide they have had enough of modern society and go live rural. Some thought they were digging humanity out of its hole, but find out that the more they learn and understand of the world, the more they realize they have gotten in so deep, it would be hard to climb back out of such a place, let along change things to improve them. Some just want a quiet and simple life.

There are many ways that people drop out of society. I'm not going to list all the ways, but I will give one simple and basic way so I can elaborate on the scenario and tell you what really happens. All other scenarios start and end almost the same way with only a few slight variations in the details, but all outcomes overall are the same.

A man is fed up with this ridiculous world. He gives away all his belongings, packs a backpack, and goes to live in a cave out in the wilderness. He lives out there in the remote wilderness for ten years survival style. He has gotten older and life starts becoming harder. He decides to come back to civilization instead of just dying out there alone. When he gets back to his hometown, things had gotten even worse than when he left. He read a newspaper, read news on the internet, watched the news on tv, all bad. He isn't surprised at all, but he is deeply saddened. He thought that some others might have tried to fight for a better future. They did not, or if they did, there weren't enough of them, or they didn't have the right method. The old man now realizes that his dropout did nothing for the world. A selfish decision he and all future generations will have to pay for. He realized that he might have been one of the only ones that knew enough about society to actually change it. He now knows that if everyone like him dropped out too, the rest of society would be too ignorant to move society forward toward a better way of life. It stayed virtually the same with only a few minor improvements in technology and equality. If all the dropouts would have stayed to fight for a better life, for more equality, better technology, and a more evolved society, maybe things could have been different in the ten years he spent.

Please don't become this old man. Stay integrated and start striving for improvements in the world. Don't give up. Don't drop out. Have you ever heard the saying, "Evil only wins when good men do nothing"? Well now would be a good time to do something. There are a lot of things even one person that doesn't have a lot of free time can do. That is why I came up with the idea The TimeLordz Movement! One person can only do so much with the time they have, but if that person was able to free up 2 to 10 bright and highly motivated people, that group has a higher probability of improving the world around them. Then, taking things nation wide on a larger scale, If there were just 100,000 timelords able to give ten people each food,shelter,water, and electricity, then we would have 1,000,000 fierce and talented individuals, who's full time job is to improve and evolve the world and society. I bet good things would come for everyone within ten years if we had a million people fighting for this. Future generations would be pleased to say the least. Timelords is a hope and a better way. Please fight for good things with us.

11

Ways to Become a Timelord

Now that you have a better understanding of how the world really operates, and you know the obstacles that will be on your path, you are ready to give it a try, to change the world. I will now go through many methods that a person could be a Timelord.

I'd say that there are two types of Timelords. Public and private. I know for many of you, mustering up enough courage just to try it will be hard, and you would like to still retain your own individual and family's privacy. I completely understand. I will now list all the private ways that a person can become a Timelord and share time. Then I will list more hands on and public ways.

Private timelords have a secondary dwelling outside and seperate from their family home. It could be whats called an "Accessory dwelling unit" or a guest house. You could modify a garage, or even a larger storage shed or pole barn. You could have an RV or camper. You could have a box truck, bus, uhaul, or shipping container fixed up into an rv style mobile home. You could put a trailer(mobile home) in your backyard. You could build what is called a "Yurt". A yurt is a permanent tent built on a wooden platform. Canvas or tarpaulin stretched over metal frame,pvc, or steam bent wood. You could even build a tree house. All of these methods are legal in most parts of the US. Be sure to check local zoning and ordinance rules. It will vary depending on where your property is. If you are doing well financially you could buy a duplex or multi-unit building, buy a campground or rv park. You could buy a trailer park, or big apartment building. You could buy acreage and start a "spiritual retreat" with a bunch of lodges. You can start a church camp. There are a lot of possibilities for private style Timelords. It just depends on personal preference, and what you can afford without putting yourself in too much debt or financial risk.

Public or shared living for Timelords is a bit different. You could have a roommate, or put some people in your basement. You could take a bedroom and put bunk beds in it, and put office style cubicles in your living room for their work areas. You could turn a living room, dining room, or mud/sun room into a timelords space. Just look at the space,rooms, and area of your home and write down all the possibilities, and with some creativity, you could make it a reality.

You might also want to look into forming a "Private Membership Association". It could help you and your team by protecting your rights to associate privately. There are a lot of lawyers that specialize in this sector. There are many websites and books on the subject. Look into it. It could help you.

Also research "Living Trust". It's a way to protect you and your home and assets better. Also a possible way for you to keep timelords going on indefinitely on your land even after your death.(assuming property taxes are paid and you have someone to fill your shoes to oversee operations and carry the Timelords torch)

I want to go into and give advice on recruiting, interviews, and classified ads next. When you have an area prepared and ready for timelords recruits, you will need to advertise and have interviews to find the right candidates. I recommend having an interview list with all the questions that you want to know. I would gear the questions specifically around the genre or theme that you want your Timelords to be. I would also include some questions to find out their personality traits and character. You will be investing time, resources, space, and money on your recruits, so pick very carefully. Think about it after the interviews. Like with any important decision, sleep on it and give it a couple of days to have a more clear mind. I also recommend creating a contract that states all the rules of the house, and possibly make them a "day to day basis guest". Don't let them give you any money, and don't let them change address or receive mail there. Also put in the contract that if they violate any of the rules of the house or contract, they will be forced to leave with 24hr notice. You want to do all these things so you don't get stuck with an "actor looking for a handout" or a "sabotager". Otherwise you would have to evict them with the court legal system. Pick your candidates well, and have them sign a guest contract that waives tenant rights and liabilities if injured and you should be fine.

The classified add to sponsor a Timelord recruit is very exciting to think about for me. I long for the day when you can get on facebook, a website or a newspaper and see these kinds of adds. "Timelord looking for three recruits for invention and innovation." or "Looking for a Timelord, my passion is zoning regulations". I will be happy and blessed that The Timelords Movement finally started when I see this stuff. Be cautious as with anything. Perform interviews at restaurants or coffee shops and other quiet public places. Do a background check and reference check to be safe. Trust your instincts and gut feelings. Have fun and enjoy the Timelords journey.

Keep in mind that the world won't change overnight. It will happen gradually. Baby steps. What is most important is that we do our best to better the world and to give future generations more equality and a higher standard of living to all. You may or may not be successful at your goals, but at least you tried. "All things are possible with time". Always keep this in mind, "We are born with nothing, and we leave this world with nothing. Life is only the journey". So try to make it a good one.

12

Cover Art Notes

The "TimeLordz Lady" is an original drawing and artwork composed by the author for this book. I want to explain some things contained within her image because I know some people will be curious about it.

Her head has the electrical field incorporated into her facial features including the eyes.

Her lips contain a heart inside to signify love radiations and emanations.

The butterfly pin means several things. It is the piezoelectric field butterfly. First discovered when charting graphs of the piezoelectric field. It symbolizes the hysteresis in the Ether. For those that don't know, the piezoelectric field is a current that flows through living things. It is crystal electricity. Since all life contains water, and once water becomes structured it contains a lattice like a crystal, thereby allowing piezoelectricity to flow through us. The butterfly is also a symbol of transformation and spiritual growth.

Her main body contains what many refer to as the magneto-dielectric field. In the hourglass shape that the fields create, I added sand to signify the sands of time. This magneto-dielectric field looks the same in humans and also in planet earth. It affects everything.

The Timelordz Movement

The TimeLordz Movement is a hope. It's a way for an average person to tip the scales in humanity's favor for more equality and a more technologically advanced civilization in the near future. To explain The Timelordz Movement simply, "A person provides food, shelter, water, and electricity to a gifted and fierce individual, thereby allowing this recruit to spend all of their time on something beneficial for humanity."
I have been studying and analyzing the world for the past twenty five years. I have seen many things over the past 43 years of my life. I have spent quite a bit of time trying to find answers on how society operates,how and why everything is set up the way it is. This book is the product of my life experience and research. In this book I put all the pieces of the puzzle together for you and then give solutions to all of our problems and shortcomings. I will give many insights into humanity's current time restraints and give solutions. By the end of the book you will have gained a deep understanding of how modern society functions and how an aspiring Timelord can use this knowledge to upgrade and change the world around them.

www.ingramcontent.com/pod-product-compliance
Lightning Source LLC
Chambersburg PA
CBHW060531280326
41933CB00014B/3137